THE BIG THREE

THREE WAYS YOUR SPIRIT IS TRYING TO GET YOUR ATTENTION AND HOW TO GET BACK INTO THE FLOW

ZALAH

Copyright © 2021 by Zalah

All rights reserved.

I am hesitant to put a copyright on this material because I believe that spiritual information should be freely shared for the benefit of all of humanity as it has been without copyright as in The Bible, The Quran, The Vedas, The Tripitaka (The Buddhist Scriptures) and more. However, to prevent use by those with the intent to misuse or misinterpret this information, I have consented to copyright this work to protect the integrity of the message and to allow for it to be shared freely with permission from the author. That being said, no part of this book may be reproduced in any form or by any electronic or mechanical means, including information storage and retrieval systems, without written permission from the author, except for the use of brief quotations in a book review.

Category: BODY, MIND & SPIRIT / Mindfulness & Meditation, SELF-HELP / Personal Growth / General, SELF-HELP / Spiritual, PHILOSOPHY / Mysticism

Cover design by Ziterah Loudon

Cover Image from Pexels

Book design by Melanie Johnston

All quotations remain the intellectual property of their respective originators. All use of quotations is made under the fair use copyright principle.

ISBN: 978-1-7776254-1-2

Published by The Centre For Transformation

www.TheCFT.ca

ACKNOWLEDGMENTS

∼

First and foremost, I wish to thank my beloved God for this life and all that you have taught me directly and indirectly through my Master Teacher, on this metaphysical plane, many years ago. I could never thank you both enough. My Divine partnership with you, My God, has brought me to tears so many times and to this moment in life where I can share some of what I have been taught. It has been a humbling experience getting here.

Let me also acknowledge this is not my teaching. "The Teaching" is based on "The Wisdom of the Ages." I do not own The Teaching, other than I own it by increasingly living it to the best of my abilities and I assure you, it has been humbling. I advise students that The Teaching does not change you, rather it reveals who you are and what your values are.

I would also like to acknowledge and to Divinely thank my two earth angels, Ziterah Loudon and Melanie Johnston.

Your tireless work and efforts on this book and so many other projects are deeply appreciated. I thank you for bringing me to this point and being my Divine workhorses. Each of you has demonstrated incredible and sustained Divine kindness, commitment, support, and foresight for me. Angels do live and breathe. I recognize the effort and dedication you have committed to compile this information and get it onto these pages; you both were instrumental in creating this book.

I cannot thank you enough.

Also, a big thank you to Alandria Hales for your diligent efforts in transcribing many of my teaching talks. You spent countless hours doing whatever needed to be done and you have my sincere gratitude.

God Bless

∼

CONTENTS

Preface	vii
Introduction	xi
1. FINDING AUTHENTIC MEANING IN LIFE	1
Focus	2
Life & Love	5
Presence And Now Moments	8
G.O.D.	11
The Act	14
2. HOW AND WHY YOUR SPIRIT IS TRYING TO GET YOUR ATTENTION & THE BIG THREE	17
Getting Lost In The Illusion	17
S.H.I.T. (Spiritually Harmonizing Intelligent Truth)	19
THE BIG THREE	21
The Big Three: Relationships	23
The Big Three: Finances	26
The Big Three: Health	31
3. WHAT CAN YOU DO TO GET BACK INTO THE DIVINE FLOW?	37
The Way Out Is By Going Within: Meditation	38
Don't Judge	42
Harmonize, Harness, and Convert	45
The Tools To Evolve	47
Integrity	50
Life Happens For Us, Not To Us	51
Conscious Choices	54
Your Power Is In Your Peace	56
Childlike Properties	58
Being The Observer	59
The Inside World	62
Your Opportunity Is Here, Now	64

About the Author 69
Also by Zalah 73

PREFACE

∼

COVID-19

As this book was written, COVID-19 began to seriously surface and take over much of the world's conversation and focus. It is waning in some areas with the introduction of various vaccines, however there are now concerns about the new variants of COVID-19. Hopefully, we all have learned how valuable life and Mother Nature are in the COVID pause. COVID-19 has brought so many to question life at the very core of their belief structures and to contemplate, and sometimes realize, their worst fears. It has left people questioning their beliefs, values, and perspectives. So many are calling out and asking why nothing seems to make sense anymore. Whatever you believe as to the virus's seriousness, you are right.

Whether you believe in the legitimacy of COVID-19 or not, there is no question as to its negative impact on the economies of the world, families, and individuals. It is taxing personal relationships (right through to divorces) which are compounded

Preface

by the degradation of human health in various degrees (right down to death).

It is my opinion that COVID-19 is the catalyst of a great recalibration and transformation for society in general. At this moment, I believe the recalibration of society has just started, and another COVID-19 resurgence may occur if we, the human race, have not learned our lessons of sacred respect for our own Divinity, for each other, and of course, Mother Nature. The important positive by-product is that COVID-19 has provided Mother Nature with an opportunity to inhale.

Life is a great thing... if it doesn't kill you. That is one of the great paradoxes of life. How many times have you got slammed hard enough by life to stop you dead in your tracks, only to look up at the sky and ask, "What?? Why???" Well, hang onto your hat as the full body slam for society (in mass) is now happening. Now this can take your breath away as you begin to understand what is going on—and why this mega re-calibration is occurring here on the planet, at this time.

This is the time for the soulful quantum leap you came to this planet for, where you can fully wake up. It is game time as 'The Divine Flip' is about to happen. It's about realizing your own soulful integrity courtesy of COVID-19.

COVID-19 is the facilitator of transformation of The Big Three in almost everyone's life on this planet. It is affecting everyone in different degrees of severity. It is re-calibrating everything in society... including you.

The Big Three are Relationships, Health, and Finances—all of which are being stretched and stressed to the limits, in varying degrees, for almost everyone on a global scale. As this happens in one, two or three areas of your life, you must squirt up the middle to Spirit to connect to your Source. This is actually an opportunity for you to evolve if you can see it.

Preface

Take these words sacredly and understand why it is happening, right here, right now.

If you have had enough of the challenges, struggle, and pain, and just want to make sense out of your life and the world around you, keep reading. It will help you make sense out of life and perhaps see your world in a new light.

INTRODUCTION

∼

THIS IS A SMALL BOOK WITH HUGE, SIMPLE, SPIRITUAL TRUTHS

Have you ever wondered why the same challenges keep showing up in your life over and over and over again? Do you get frustrated by never seeming to get ahead, and for the life of you, you can't figure out what life is really all about? Is it possible that all of the challenges and roadblocks in your life have been Divinely orchestrated to get you to go within and reconnect with your Source so that you can finally find your way?

If you don't go within... you will go without what you really want.

Well, the first section of this book is about life actually happening *for* you... not to you.

I know, that's a real shocker to some people. Your Spirit is constantly *whispering*—sometimes **shouting**—to get your

Introduction

attention, and it usually shows up in three key parts of your life.

This book is about identifying those three big areas of life where Spirit is nudging you or outright grinding you down to get your attention. It gives you some tools you can use to create your way out of what you perceive to be the less-than-optimal circumstances in your life. Those areas of your life where you say "SHIT!" are actually gifts to help you evolve. This word has a spiritual meaning (believe it or not) that we will cover in this book.

It's just a matter of how you look at your "S.H.I.T." and whether you choose to respond to it and learn from it or keep reacting and stay stuck in that pattern for a lifetime. It is also about looking at your life through a different lens to help you see the gifts and tools you have been given to help you navigate life. You just never realized they were in your toolbox before now.

The second section is about The Big Three. Before we get there, there are some essential concepts of life in the first section that I would like to share with you in perhaps a different way than how you have understood them in the past. These foundational concepts are vital to your spiritual evolution in this lifetime.

For example, "Divine", heart-centered, and unconditional "Love". The Love that flows through you from "The Source" and is the essence of who you truly are. Contemplating life through that lens of Love allows you to see things from a different perspective when you read about The Big Three. Once you realize that life is trying to show you something, you can STOP, NOT REACT to it, and OBSERVE the problem from a neutral and loving space, then RESPOND and get the lesson that life is showing you, and finally move through it.

As I have said, the focus of this book is about The Big Three. It is about where we all get caught in any or all three of these dynamics and how each of these dynamics feed each other. And

Introduction

why life can be so incredibly challenging and exhausting, especially if you don't get the big picture. Having one, two or all three of these dynamics in play keeps you in a state of constant unrest and can typically stress every area of your life, to death. It soon becomes very clear as to why you feel stuck in fear and are increasingly anxious and/or depressed. Within that uncomfortable feeling and the restlessness of knowing that there must be something more to life, is your opportunity to see what is really happening and, if we are all going to go through this, we might as well "grow" through it.

Finally, in the third section of this book, we will talk about the tools to help you begin to get clear of what has held you back and kept you stuck. You can start to use these tools to convert and transform your life and to find meaning in what is being shown to you. Life begins to make sense again and you may realize that there really is a purpose for all you have gone through. Perhaps then, authentic magic, joy and a feeling of freedom will appear or re-appear in your life.

I believe intuitively that we all know there is more to life than the day-to-day grind; that there is a never-ending source of Love, Integrity and Peace in the Universe. All that is missing is your awareness of how to get in tune with it to help you navigate and fully enjoy life. I am not saying that nothing will ever collapse or go sideways again. I am saying there are simple tools that will help you begin to move through these times with grace and ease. They will help you embrace life and the lessons you are being shown so you can advance spiritually, mentally, and physically.

So, let's take a journey together to help you change your perception of life so that you can get unstuck and find true and deep meaning again. When you change the way you look at things, the things you look at change.

1

FINDING AUTHENTIC MEANING IN LIFE

∽

This book is about the three big areas of life that your Spirit (Oversoul, Higher Self) is typically wearing you down in to try to get your attention to get back in tune with your Spirit. Within these pages, you will find a very different guidebook for life from what you have learned in the past.

It has what seem to be very simple concepts. But in reality, living these ideas to their fullest potential is no easy feat. In fact, it takes a very strong soul to contemplate, accept, and then adopt some of these thoughts and ideas into daily life. If you do, I guarantee your life will begin to transform in ways you never thought possible. It takes commitment and hard work, but if you use the knowledge, disciplines, and perceptions you learn here, your life will change.

You see, our lives were never meant to be a bother; rather they are meant to be a series of opportunities and challenges to get us to understand why we are experiencing them and what we can learn from them, and that we can create our way out of them.

We are, in fact, beings of creation. We were created to create! We have long forgotten that and have seemingly given up on understanding what a grand adventure life can be. We have settled for the same old grind with little meaning and even less satisfaction. Within these pages, may you find the path to the life you have always dreamed of creating.

So, let this be your guide to understanding your life a little better and allow it to bring some light and a breath of fresh air into your world.

Let's start with some key elements of an optimized life.

Focus

Life goes through phenomenal phases and if you haven't noticed, you are probably going through an anxiety phase at this very moment.

What if I told you that there is an energy wave currently pouring through the Universe, and therefore the planet, that magnifies where you are at. Within this energy wave dynamic, there is something that you are feeling (a little to a lot anxious) about, without knowing exactly what it is. If you are filled with fear, guilt, shame, anxiety, worry or a variety of emotions, it can be very tough right now as these are magnified on the planet and are possibly just 'driving you crazy.' The only safe place is Peace and Love as they are conducive to your spiritual growth.

Fear, anxiety, and feeling like you are losing control are the telltale signs that you have lost your spiritual connection. You see, fear and anxiety are part of the personality whereas Love is of the soul. So, if you are feeling fear, which is usually a bedfellow of anxiety, then you are at the doorway of your opportunity to change your reality.

The Big Three

Now how do you change your reality? Well, all advanced spiritual teachers know the formula, and here it is:

• your Reality is determined by your Thoughts and Actions,

• your Thoughts and Actions are determined by your Consciousness,

• your Consciousness is determined by the amount of Presence that you have,

• the amount of Presence that you have is determined by the Quality of your Meditations.

What do I mean by the quality of your meditations? Well, it's kind of like the senior monk who, with a wink and a smile, says to his senior initiate, "I've never met such a thoughtless person as you." We regard thoughtless as inconsiderate but actually thoughtless can be an ideal state of "Being" if you think about it in this context.

Can you get to a thoughtless state of mind?

That's what I mean by the quality of your meditations. If you are sitting meditating for 45 minutes to an hour, ideally the first 15 minutes should only be about what I call the "Illusion" or the "S.C.O.P.E." of your life (stuff, circumstances, occasions, persons, experiences). This is the "scope" you view your life through.

Everything in the physical world is unreal, which is why it is called the Illusion. The Illusion is comprised of all the stuff (S.C.O.P.E.) that you will leave behind when you pass on after this life has ended. This is the stuff that your "Ego/Act" wants to distract you with while you are trying to meditate. If you get caught thinking about the Illusion for the entire time, you haven't truly had a quality meditation.

To avoid this, when you start meditating consistently, set your intention so that beyond the first 15 minutes, your meditation is about going to the "Void", "Pure Spirit"—that blue-black vastness of space, and hanging out there as long as you can.

The Void is your ultimate goal to get to when you are meditating. It is that place where you become timeless and endless. Your goal is to become thoughtless in the Void—that place of vast "Nothingness". The Void is where masters, for centuries, have gone to create their realities. The best of everything comes from Nothing!

In meditation, while in the Void (which is Nothing physically, yet *all* things potentially), just idealize sitting there and becoming Present as a 'thoughtless' person, as an optimized way of connecting and being. This is quite a concept—to merge with the place you originally came from—Spirit. This all happens through deep Presence.

And people in your life will ask you, "What do you do?"

And you could one day say, "Oh Nothing, I'm a thoughtless person."

"Really?" they'll say. "Did you have to work at that?"

And with a subtle, quiet smile, you'll reply, "You have no idea!"

Yet in a social context, to be thoughtless is highly disdained. People may say, "Oh, how inconsiderate you must be if you are such a thoughtless person,"... Ouch! As you can see, that is a much different context than what I am discussing here.

We have become over-agitated in our lives with regards to the Illusion (S.C.O.P.E.). Being over-agitated is not a very effective way of life, and you will find that you have no focus.

Focus is about being able to concentrate on one thing for a set period of time. Focus is the absence of dualistic thought. Can you hold one thought for a minute? Because if I train you, you will understand why you would want to idealize focusing on one thought and not all the combinations and permutations thereof. ***Just one thought***. And then if I can get you to do that, I can get you to consider possibly thinking of Nothing... which, if sustained impeccably, is a prerequisite to creating at will.

Most people I have trained over the years, especially business executives, think that focusing on one thought would be impossible. Bear with me here. I can teach you to think about Nothing without falling asleep. Most people realize that if I could teach them to do this it would really be something. For many people, the mind is a terrible place, and it is best to not go there alone.

A lot of people are afraid of silence and yet that is where our true power lies—in sustained silence. When you get in the car with some people, they're thinking, "Let's not have any long periods of silence; turn on that radio, or let's keep chatting." They don't have the emotional maturity or spiritual security to sustain long periods of silence when really, that is where your growth is, in silence.

~

Life & Love

Life is a phenomenal thing—if it doesn't kill you.

You live your life and then cross back over to the other half of the sky when your time on Earth is done. When you go back to the other half of the sky, many entities that haven't visited this half of the sky will ask you, "How was it?" And you will possibly say like I do, "Life in duality in the Illusion? There's nothing like it!"

How do you possibly explain life in duality, in the Illusion, to an entity that has never been here? The truth is, you can't. You have to experience it. Experience is truth.

What is duality? All things in the physical Illusion are made up of atoms. An atom is made up of positively charged protons and negatively charged electrons, so it follows that every 'thing', all matter, is made up of positive and negative charges. The world of opposites also includes other cascading aspects, such as emotions, thoughts, experiences, and relationships. As humans, we get caught in duality by rationalizing back and forth between the stimulation of life's circumstances and the reactions to those events. To rise above duality, to participate and live life from a space of Divine Love, leads to joy.

The incredible part is that you get charged with Divine Love on the other half of the sky before you come into this life. But the more confused you get in life and drain those Love reserves while you are here, the more insane you become because Love is sanity. It's that simple. Have you ever paid attention to that moment when the bond is broken with somebody that you love? Either through a partnership dissipating or death, you know that moment where you start to feel that the love is not there anymore? You really, really have clarity through contrast in that moment. When you realize the human love is not there, you go temporarily insane for a while. It's sad, but it is very true because pure Love is sanity.

Love is also a key component when you are assisting others. That is probably when you are at your best. You do so, not just for your own sanity and to feel good, but in terms of the Love that other people need to receive. You are at an access point to Spirit when you are able to give and live from your heart with Love. You cannot give more love than you already have, much like you can't write a check for more than you have in your bank account. You simply can't give away more than what you have. In order to really understand that, you will want to keep filling yourself up with Love so that you have more to give.

The Big Three

Many people think that the more people give, the less that they have, but it's just the reverse. The more you give away, the more you can get. But do not give so much that you lose your Divine Self and connection. If you lose your Divine Self and Love connection, you have to be able to go back to Source and replenish yourself before you can give more and more Love again and again.

"It's like in The Teachings," I say to students. "Some come to drink at the fountain of knowledge... others come to gargle. And some will outright come to swim in the waters of love and truth." I make light of this because, over the years, people come and go. They study and wake up to a certain degree, and then they fade off for a while and sometimes come back again. They rise to the level of what it is that they need to own in their life and the Illusion, and sometimes it's too hard for them. They are not prepared to own what they need to own until they build the courage to try again. So they just go away. Everyone in life rises to their point of failure. Life really is about understanding Love and living life with courage.

So again, Love is sanity. We get lost on this half of the sky because we are not tethered to Love in a pure way, continually. We get compromised in various dynamics, we get confused, and we lose our Divine way which is Love. Human love is typically emotional love, and it has its ups and downs. Divine Love is an energy—it is not an emotion. So, can you get above the human love and tap into that Divine Love inherent within you? Can you get above your challenges and Love in the face of it all, whether someone or certain circumstances are making you happy or sad? That is the question—can you get above the conditions?

Actually, life is all about Love first, will second. You must continually expand both.

The bottom line is that Love is the beingness of all things.

Love is space.

Love is an energy.

Love is in this world, but not of this world.

∽

Presence And Now Moments

Life is what happens to you when you are busy making plans.

Before you wake up in life and find its true value, usually a few decades have gone by. You have probably had the experience that I did as a child, where time felt really long, especially summer vacation. I would say to my best friend, "What do you want to do?"

And he would say, "I don't know, what do you want to do?"... and we would keep repeating this back and forth. We would always laugh. Time was sooo long in innocence.

It seemed like there were summers back then that were longer than decades of my life now. Why was that? It was because of the childlike properties that were inherent within us at the time. Properties like Divine Love, Innocence, Presence, Being the Observer (non-judgment), Light-heartedness and Trust. When you have childlike properties, time expands and you are naturally in the now. In childhood, there was so much of "what do you want to do?" It was an incredibly beautiful time of life. I am sure that this dynamic was typical of so many childhood relationships as time felt like it could go on forever. Then adulthood came with all of its choices, dynamics and compromising situations.

I remember telling my teenage son, who is a doctor now, "You'll see when you get older, time flies faster."

The Big Three

And he said, "Dad, come on, a measured metric of time is a proven unit of time; it doesn't vary."

"Really?" I said. "Talk to me when you have four or five decades under your belt. You will see that as you get older, time flies faster. If you think the last twenty or thirty years have flown by fast, the next twenty will go by even faster."

So, what truly matters in life? I'll tell you what matters – Presence! Moments of Love and Presence in life. "Now" moments. That love you have for the special people of your life. The moments when you had no other thought of any other things but that moment. Perhaps it was during the birth of a child, the death of a loved one, or when a serious accident occurred. Now moments are your key memories of life when you have no other thoughts of any other thing. This is being present.

If someone you love was to die tomorrow, or *you* were to die tomorrow, what do you wish you would have said? What do you wish you would have done? And why are you not doing that now? Why are you not telling someone that you love them? Inviting them to lunch? Having long conversations with them? Why aren't you doing these things with the people that matter? Why don't you do something out of the ordinary?

If you do something out of the ordinary with those special people, it's called being extraordinary. To have extraordinary moments in your life, you will have to do *extra-ordinary* things. What are you not doing now that, if the opportunity was gone (either that person left your life, or you left the planet), you wish you would have said and done? Phone someone up today and tell them how much you love them. Have tea, have a few laughs, because we only have each other on loan for a little while on this planet.

If someone were to call you to connect, even if it was inconvenient, it should never be a bother. It should be an honor because those are the extraordinary moments of your life. If you want an extraordinary life, it is contingent on you respecting life and doing extra ordinary things on occasion and building on that. People will love you even more when you do this, and do you know why? You did something extraordinary for them. You got up really early or in the middle of the night, and you gave them something that brought a tear to their eye. Presence. You cupped their face and said, "I love you, I love you. I've been asleep here and I have never told you how much I love you."

They will probably say, "Is something wrong?"

And your response may be, "No—something just got right."

Maybe it is your focused Presence with your Mom or Dad. Perhaps it's a spouse, a child, a relative, or a friend. You know what? Your life is measured by these moments that take your breath away. It is not the *quantity* of life that you live, it is the *quality* of life. Presence. If you understand this key value, your life changes. The magic of life is in Presence.

As Max Plank (a very prominent physicist) originally said, "When you change the way you look at things, the things you look at change." In doing that, you are looking at the opportunity that you have while you are here on this half of the sky. Because when you go back to the other half of the sky, it is for life review and rest. You don't evolve on that half of the sky. You evolve on this half, only through experience. Life is where experience is, and experience is truth. You rest on the other half of the sky, then you may come back and experience life again if you choose to.

Presence is about pre-sense. You have a lot of natural Presence through Divine connection, intuition and through mindfulness, which were all abundant when you were a child. You pre-sensed when something was about to happen. This intuition gets disconnected as you grow older because the Illusion's polarized dynamics become a priority in your life as you age. You can become very disconnected and even lost in the Illusion to various depths. You become filled with fear, guilt, shame, worry, pain, loss, and anxiety.

The mechanics of consciousness—including imagination—don't work optimally without Sacred Presence and Love. Presence is the most sacred consciousness tool and is essential for a fertile mind. This sacredness starts with your mindfulness and your sacred respect for life in general, and all things in it. Sacredness is an absolute prerequisite for Presence and this leads to Peace of Being. These concepts are all inextricably linked together.

∼

G.O.D.

First and foremost, GOD is Love. And Love is the beingness of all things.

Love is in all of us and is the very core of our being, irrespective of gender. Love is universal.

That of which is *not* in tune with Love must fall away.

Love resists nothing, yet conquers all.

So this teaching is not about religion; it is about Spirit. It is not my teaching—I am just a copper wire, the conduit. I just teach it. It is my truth, and I live it at the highest level that I possibly can. Am I perfect? No. Was Jesus perfect? No. Was Buddha? No. People have misinformed images of master teachers that are contorted. Did Jesus get emotional? Yes. If you study the Bible, he caught the money changers on the steps of the Sacred place of worship and grabbed them by the scruff of the neck and said, "Get out of here. This is a sacred place." I am paraphrasing here, but you get the picture.

This teaching is about practical spirituality. It is based in meditation, but not on any religion. Many have left religion and found God anyway. For me, God is the

Grand
Over-all
Designer

Many have found their Higher Selves with the assistance of religion. There is *no one way* to connect and evolve. As the saying goes, there are many roads to Rome.

A seasoned teacher will show you where your old neural nets of limited perceptions, beliefs and habits are. These are well-worn paths you do not even know exist until they are shown to you in the mirrors of life. Now, if I am going to get you to think differently, you have to take conscious steps off the path of your old neural nets.

It is like creating a new pathway in a cornfield that is half grown, which is a little more difficult than walking on the well-worn path on the grass of your existing unconscious ways. So you have to take each focused conscious step along this new path of thinking differently. It involves a lot of trust, and you have to be focused on thinking this new way, looking for the best in life through all your stuff, circumstances, occasions, persons, and experiences (S.C.O.P.E.). If you look for the best, it stops the judging. Why? Because you start looking for the best versus how you are going to be taken advantage of. You need to stop this way of thinking. And if you don't want to stop, I will ask you, "How did that old way of thinking work for you? How well did you do?"

You do not see the world as it is; you see the world as you are!

The Big Three

You may be thinking, "But will I be taken advantage of by not looking for where I could get cheated?" Yep, you are going to get taken advantage of every once in a while; however, in the balance of things, what you lose in one part of life, you will more than make up for in another. And you are going to love the end result —which is sanity. You will love this new place that you will be at, as Love is sanity. You now have a prescription that eliminates confusion. There is no confusion in integrity, and Love is integrity. You will not be lost in life if you are living with integrity. Integrity produces Peace.

Peace is where it really is at, especially right now on this planet, and in your life.

Ultimate Love = Ultimate Integrity = Ultimate Peace

The Teaching is about you understanding that God is not having you think about figuring it out, God has already done that and you just need to trust and keep yourself in integrity. Now that is a simple, yet profound, way of being if you get it. Profound! God's already figured it out and it is for you to align yourself with Spirit. Align yourself to truth. The door to truth is always open. It is a matter of each of us choosing to walk through it. Trust and Presence are the keys.

So, you think you are reading this by accident? You wanted clarity someplace along the line, and your "Oversoul (your Higher Self, your Spirit)" said, "This book is for you." This little book will help you to connect with your purpose... your Higher Self. The process of connecting with your Higher Self is greatly enhanced with sustained contemplation, stillness, and silence... especially when in nature.

I do my best to help make sense out of life, because for many, the load of life is just too much, especially right now.

The Act

Now, let's talk about your "Act." Everyone has one, more or less.

The Act or Ego is used interchangeably and in simple terms, this will help you understand its true nature. As Dr. Wayne Dyer wrote, EGO stands for **E**dging, **G**od, **O**ut.

The Act is who you think you are in the Illusion while living in dualism; it is not the real you.

Think of the Act as your human identity. The complexity of the Act encompasses all of these life dynamics: your employment, education, house, car, reputation, friends, status, image, and ego. It is a person's rational way of existing in the Illusion and therefore, it wants to be right always and in all ways. One problem... the Act does not survive your death.

At its root, the Act is fear-based and most often triggers a person to react to life with fear. It wants to always be right. Generally, you hold onto your Act as a form of surviving through life, not realizing there is so much more to experience. The Act is all about "doing" stuff—the "To Do" lists that bind you to the Illusion on a daily, weekly, monthly, yearly and lifetime's continuum. As such, you become unconscious or asleep spiritually via the habits that tie you to the limited human part of your existence—the Illusion and all of the S.C.O.P.E. (stuff, circumstances, occasions, persons and experiences).

The Act typically looks for what is wrong. It serves to keep you bound to form in this Illusion, a prisoner and as such, you are unable to access your true Self, your Spirit.

Again, be aware that the Act does not survive your death and is usually only used as a yardstick of measurement for your life in the Illusion.

The Big Three

Understand that the size of your human drama is the size of your Act. You can get beyond your Act and get enhanced access to your Spiritual Being by meditating, especially if you meditate in nature. Our society generally does not introduce or support essential awareness or development of our true Self, our Oversoul. Society, at least western society, has a major focus on the Act development. This causes many people to get caught permanently in the Act. Another book of mine, <u>Caught in the Act</u>, describes my own experience with being caught in the Act.

The Act stands as a centurion at the prison gate, directing the illusory concepts such as acceptance or non-acceptance, like or dislike, and judgment or non-judgment as primary realities. The Act is very clever. It has many cloaks and costumes and can even disguise itself from itself. When the Act is examined in this role, it uses the dialogue of form to convince the human that there is only one reality, the one the Act is invested in, and that there is no other reality.

The worst kind of Act is the Spiritual Act. Just when you feel you are connected and understand spiritual principles logically, the Act may consider itself as the spiritual link and thus responsible for all Divine knowledge. To truly be connected is to live the dance of collaboration with your Spirit; it is not a memorized or logic-based way of being.

One way to curb the Act is to sit in silent meditation until the chatter stops. This could take dedication over a very long period of time (it could take years to stop the chatter if meditating daily, depending how deeply you are polluted by the Illusion). Those who meditate in nature are able to quiet the chatter in less time. A near-death experience (NDE) will also generally also overcome the Act. An NDE is not something that is brought about voluntarily, but by the Oversoul.

We are all here to get beyond the Act in the Illusion. In a Divine sense, we are each helping those we meet to get to where we need to be by serving as mirrors for each other. We are all walking each other home. Look at each individual from the point of view of what is right and not what is wrong. Look to see if each individual you encounter is offering a lesson or a gift for you.

Your true Self, your Oversoul, physically anchors within your heart (the fourth seal or chakra). With awareness, Presence and by living life consciously and lovingly from the heart, you can avoid getting permanently trapped in your Act within a lifetime.

Now that we've covered some of the basics of life that we all experience daily, you may begin to see life with fresh eyes and allow that knowledge to become the foundation for you to grow and evolve in this lifetime. These key elements can be your compass to an optimized life if you so choose.

2

HOW AND WHY YOUR SPIRIT IS TRYING TO GET YOUR ATTENTION & THE BIG THREE

∼

Before we get into the Big Three dynamics in life, let's look at places where we all seem to get caught up in life, time after time, after time.

∼

Getting Lost In The Illusion

What do I mean by "The Illusion?" Well, everything in material form eventually goes back to no-thing, Nothing, or Spirit. Material form is temporary, and the Illusion is a misconstrued perception of what is truly real. Nothing real can be destroyed. Your Spirit and Soul are truly real and cannot be destroyed. Everything in the physical world is unreal; therefore, it is called the Illusion. The gift of the Illusion is that it is the stepping stone to your Divinity; the Illusion is here for your evolution and your enlightenment. You typically find out who you are by who you are not. The Illusion is instrumental in distinguishing that.

You must be able to remember Love in the middle of the Illusion. For most people, this is like remembering advice your Mom gave you at home before you find yourself in the middle of an amusement park. There are so many sights and smells and colors and things to do. There is *so much*; it is overwhelming. And you know that if you don't *pay attention*, you will get lost in the "so much." This is how we fall out of the flow of Love and Presence. We seldom stop and check-in and ask ourselves, "What would Love do now?"

In life, we get lost because there is so much volume coming at us. The volume that causes this anxiety and fear is made for you to find your center. It is all made for you to go within. It is actually your opportunity to sit and meditate and connect with your Spirit to learn why you are being shown what it is that life is showing you. If you do not go within, you are going to go without a lot of things in life. Go, sit in nature, in the trees (in a safe place and preferably in the middle of the night). If you do this long enough and consistently enough while looking at the sky, over months and years you will get to your center!

If you do not go within, you will go without. It's a coin with two sides and you have to understand that. One side is if you don't go within, you are going to go without your dreams. Things just won't work out because, if all your dreams were to come true, most likely you would not have the time to go within and connect with your Oversoul.

The other side is if you don't go within, you will go without your spiritual connection, which is everyone's primary purpose in life —to reconnect. You will not question, contemplate and connect with your Oversoul if you are totally satisfied with your Illusion. You would miss the opportunity to create your life from the space of Presence, Peace, and Love that I have talked about. That is why some prayers should not be answered.

The Big Three

So, between the Act and getting lost in a wild adventure of the Illusion, how does your Oversoul get a hold of you? Let's look at that next.

∽

S.H.I.T. (Spiritually Harmonizing Intelligent Truth)

I have said if you don't go within and engage your Higher Self to guide you in life, you are going to go without. Which means you are going to get buried in the Illusion. The idea is *not* to be buried by it but rather use it as a guide to help you grow and develop. Typically, you are out there in the Illusion absorbing all of its dynamics of your S.C.O.P.E. like everybody does. You forget your Higher Self and you become disconnected. That was and *is* the original sin. In that disconnection is where your anxiety, depression, discomfort and other dynamics and dramas occur. This is where the proverbial shit hits the fan. It's where the real shit occurs in life.

The true acronym S.H.I.T. stands for Spiritually, Harmonizing, Intelligent, Truth. True teachers know what real S.H.I.T. is in life and that it is inevitable. It is the mechanism that helps you evolve. It is the Universe trying to tell you something through Spiritually Harmonizing Intelligent Truth that you are just not seeing. Perhaps over and over and over again.

Most people damn their S.H.I.T. If you are smart, you look and become conscious of what the Universe has been trying to tell you that you are not getting. The S.H.I.T. keeps coming out of that big pipeline, and until you get it, you are buried in S.H.I.T.

Typically, you are not getting what "you want" in life; however, you need to understand you are getting what "you need", from an evolutionary standpoint. It is a matter of you understanding it and capitalizing upon it through the principle of Harmonize,

Harness and Convert (H.H.C. – I will expand on this concept later in the book). You are not going to get around it; you must go through it. If not, it will keep reoccurring in more taxing and challenging ways. Going through it is a very humbling exercise but worth it for your evolution – if you get it. If you are going to "go through it," you may as well "grow through it."

If you continue to not get it, you give up because you are not listening to and learning from the S.H.I.T. that is occurring. You do not get it and if you are complaining, *you really don't get it*. It is all meant to have you go within. Now, how much more of this S.H.I.T. can you take is the question? A mature spiritual teacher will ask you that very question. Right now, the Universe is turning up the volume of the S.H.I.T pipeline in almost everyone's life – it's not just you. It is where you need to evolve. Interestingly, S.H.I.T. does not stick to Love. So, if you are in a place of Divine Love and Peace, you will convert that S.H.I.T. much sooner (rather than later).

The truth shall set you free, but first, I think it gives you a little brain damage before you get it. That's my perception based on my own experience, and experience is truth. It's a funny thing; you are led to what you need to know and/or what you call out for when the time is right. This is how people are led to me as a teacher. They find their teacher when they finally get to the point where they are ready and think, 'Can anybody make any sense of all of this? It's driving me crazy. I can't enjoy life!' You are probably applying this information to your personal circumstances right now, and hopefully, it provides some helpful insights.

As I said, the truth shall set you free, so how much more of this S.H.I.T. can you handle before you start to convert it? I can teach you how to convert your S.H.I.T. so that your life becomes joy-full, especially if you want to live a life of peace and harmony.

The Big Three

If not, the definition of insanity applies which is doing the same thing over and over again and expecting a different result.

Perhaps now you can view the S.H.I.T. of your life constructively and use it positively for your evolution. Enjoy your S.H.I.T. It is a rite of passage in the sea of duality.

THE BIG THREE

Your S.H.I.T is like a ringing phone from Spirit, and it usually comes in three types of rings—what I call The Big Three.

The Big Three are three areas of life that contain events that range from slight challenges to outright disasters. Most people have to go through these to wake them up from the Illusion they are living in order to connect with their Higher Selves.

The Big Three are Relationships, Finances and Health

Generally, a person has to get knocked down a few times in life in one or all of these areas before asking, "What is this life all about?" Now typically, these Big Three can come in line one after another or two at a time. If you have a really tough, stubborn human caught in their Act (Ego), The Big Three can come all at the same time. At this point, the person is getting hammered and they don't know whether to turn right or left. This state can be utterly paralyzing.

If you haven't noticed before, relationships, financial situations, and health are a real struggle for many at the moment because very few people understand the big squeeze we are all experiencing right now. Most fail to recognize the importance of getting to and staying in their spiritual center.

It is as though the Universe is saying, "There is a whole different reality shift that has to happen for this planet to survive." It is like we are all cells in the body of God. We need to become healthy. If each one of us finds our spiritual center, personal pollution in our collective human psyche gets cleared up, and as we clean up our own human lives by finding our center, the planet's pollution will clear up as a result. It does not take 100% of the population to do this, but it will take a significant portion to start. Until then, the pressure in the pressure cooker will increase.

The only way out of this mess is by going within to our spiritual center. Otherwise, confusion increases within each of our worlds, and disharmony occurs over and over as the dynamics cascade over each other. The only safe place right now is Peace and Love.

We are all going to have to let go of what we think we want in the Illusion and of what we perceive would be a more perfect life. We must shift our focus to become connected to our spiritual center. We must learn how to shift our priorities and just to BE.

The first sin (spiritually speaking and not religiously) was and is separation. We became separated because we started putting the Illusion first, shortly after we were born. Our parents endorsed this, and separation began. I am talking about separation from Spirit, the Oversoul.

Why does this happen? Most people on this planet were born to parents who never taught us that the inside world is much more important than the outside world of man-made things. Our parents should have repeated this over and over to us as a child so that we would never forget our connection to our Higher Selves. Now for many, this means trying to unscramble scrambled eggs because they just cannot comprehend what they can do to get back to that place of connection and innocence and rediscover their ability to create.

∼

The Big Three: Relationships

It all starts with the first relationship between you and your God, with Spirit. As you get further invested in life, you forget to put your spiritual relationship with God (which is Love because God is Love) first. Why? Because you placed the Illusion first in your life as a priority with your S.C.O.P.E. and as life rolled on and you got older, everything made less and less sense. Slowly, things became insane. The world is experiencing this now.

If you have a shaky relationship (at best) with Spirit, chances are pretty high you have an unstable relationship with people in your life and with life itself. It's that simple. Every human relationship that you have is evidence of this. More often than not, relationships are a direct reflection of our relationship with our Higher Selves. Life is becoming recalibrated with COVID-19 as the catalyst.

As you truthfully get into intimate relationships, you will come to realize that relationships are not primarily about happiness.

They are about finding out where you are caught in your evolutionary journey and overcoming that in an intimate relationship. Any solid relationship is the union of two great forgivers. Typically, you are caught or challenged right now where you need development, healing, and clearing to ultimately find yourself in the doorway of pure Love.

Where you are caught quite often is where and what you can't see clearly—where you react, what bothers you, where you aren't entirely rational, and/or where you feel you are being wronged. More often than not you need an intimate partner to assist in identifying where it is that you are caught. These are usually traumas from childhood that you are completely unaware of. They generally run a background program that colors the way you see your life and the world. I refer to these as scotomas. These are the areas where you have a "blind spot."

Yes, you can find these things out about yourself in work relationships or friendships, but they take a lot longer and generally involve a multitude of people. The easier it is for you to run from the relationship, the harder it is for you to get to that "pay dirt" where you really hit gold in what it is you need to own or learn. Generally, it is your intimate relationships where you will consider holding onto the love to help you get through to the other side of the S.H.I.T. that comes up. You will not usually go through that difficulty or pain for a work colleague or casual acquaintance.

Where you are caught is quite often like a fishhook, snagging you. Fishhooks are notorious for being awfully hard to pull out and very painful. Being caught can be related to traumas you went through in childhood or even have to do with other lives that you do not remember. You are likely to find a pattern over time though, and you will have a particular fear-based perception that you need to grow past. And as much as it hurts and is frustrating your partner, typically it will help you both to evolve. It is about doing what is right..., not *who* is right,

It helps if someone that you love and trust can assist you in "pulling out the fishhook." Quite often, the fishhook is someplace you can't access easily. You will need someone's assistance, for the sake of time and pain, to discover and own this spot where you are caught.

The Big Three

Often, each person's fishhooks can correspond to the other person's so that both individuals are perfectly reminded of what they need to heal/clean-up/develop. The good news is, on the other side of the pain, a genuinely blissful relationship can be co-created—close to the relationship you imagined it would be like in the beginning! But to get there, you authentically have to work on yourself and transform.

In an intimate relationship, it is ideal if both of you understand this about the other and are gentle with the principles of support and challenge. You cannot be a tyrant that uses the point where you or the other person is caught as a weapon in an argument. It is about loving each other through it. That does not mean you throw your boundaries to the curb. You have to take the long view, and both parties have to be willing to take a look at themselves and do the difficult work of growing. It's always easier to blame the other person. Guess what? You would not be experiencing the relationship and what it surfaces if your Oversoul didn't think it was perfect for your growth. It is best to stand firmly in responsibility and notice your Self is providing the S.H.I.T. you need to clean up for you to create the life of your dreams and connect deeper within.

Again, relationships do not exist to make us happy; they exist to help us grow spiritually. Happiness is a by-product of successfully removing these trauma fishhooks within each other with love and kindness. In your human life, through intimate relationships, you have the opportunity to truly transform where you are caught with someone you love and trust. There is no way to happiness; happiness is the way. Ponder that for a moment. To be clear—happiness is the way to happiness.

The 'caught' experiences of your scotomas are not something that you want to share with too many people who you are not as close to. Vulnerability and laying bare your soul to grow and evolve with another person's help does not come naturally. In this intimate process, love naturally comes with incredible trust, respect with love, and being in awe of each other as you grow together into happiness.

It is a profound spiritual journey together as you come out the other end of the chaotic discord that can occur in the process of getting free of where you are caught. There really can be a light at the end of the tunnel, and it does not have to be a train. It's your Spirit!

It bears mentioning here that you really cannot love someone more than you love yourself/Self. Anything in your emotional body standing in the way of your Divine relationship will need to be cleaned up. Any human relationship that gets in the way of that Divine relationship will not work out. In the heart of it, it is actually all about you finding your way back to a deep relationship with your Oversoul. Then you can enjoy your relationships as the Love overflows from your Self and into your personal life. As you bond with your Higher Self, it will not matter what your partner triggers if you are secure in your Self Love. And in that Love-based detachment, the magic will return to your love life.

∼

The Big Three: Finances

"Money talks" is a common phrase. This is true, and for a lot of my life, money was always saying goodbye more often than hello. You soon learn in life about money; it's not how much passes through your hands, it's how much actually sticks.

Almost everyone realizes that money is the grease that helps your life move along. Without money, you come to a halt. Maybe, just maybe, that's not such a bad thing. Perhaps that gives you time to pause and reflect on the problem with more

The Big Three

focus on the answer. Life is filled with lessons, and quite often, money is one of the big couriers.

There is always a spiritual lesson to be learned with money. The first thing to learn is that worry is a prayer for what you don't want. Worry will not serve you at all.

The money lesson is typically about creativity, in other words, about creation. We don't have an economic crisis or a crisis in any other matter if we can create. However, we do have a crisis in understanding creativity and creation. You must have the mindset that you choose to create, because there is no competition in creativity.

What and who was the competition for the Wright Brothers whose first flight at Kitty Hawk made history; for Alexander Graham Bell, who engineered the telephone; for Guglielmo Marconi, who pioneered long-distance radio transmission; or Thomas Edison, who has been described as America's greatest inventor? The point is, there was little to none. However, you must start to think outside the box of your current circumstances. And if you're into creativity and creation, this becomes a spiritual matter as you partner with your Oversoul to co-create and materialize your thoughts and ideas.

To do the impossible, you must believe in the invisible, which is Spirit. As with relationships, the original sin was and is separation from your Divine power (Spirit). Again, this happened because no one ever taught us as a child that the inside world was much more important than the outside world of man-made things. As such, we got lost by putting the Illusion first and not our Spirit. This gave us a severe disconnect and serious amnesia with regards to creativity and creation. This disconnect has and still does cause a lot of confusion and pain. When I first started on the spiritual path, I can't tell you the number of times I went out in the middle of the night and looked up at the night sky and said, "Why? What do you want from me? What am I to do?"

I am sure that most people have been here at least once in their life. Quite often I didn't get my questions answered at that moment like I would have liked.

The answers did eventually come, though.

What if I told you that you were created to create?

If you are creative and in integrity with whatever you do to make a living, people will love to deal with you. If you are creative, opportunities will come. What you are looking for and who you are looking for—is also looking for you.

You need to take the time to ask, "What is life all about on this planet?" Have you possibly been here for many lifetimes? Most have on this planet. I love asking my Oversoul, "What on Earth is happening?" You would be surprised how often your Self answers back with profound knowledge. I can't say this enough: who and what you're looking for in the Illusion is looking for you. You just need to get still and silent enough to connect with that Source. You need to contemplate this because that of which you contemplate expands.

Not that I want to get religious on you, but Jesus is the one who said, "What I can do, you can do also." Now either the Master Teacher was lying or telling the truth. I choose to believe he was telling the truth. Can you imagine creating things out of thin air – right out of the blue? Yet, how many of us actually spend time imagining having precisely that ability? Not many! You were created to create. We all create consciously or unconsciously. If you like the thought of creating consciously, then the trick is devoting enough time to repetitively, deeply imagining that ability to create. As Albert Einstein said, "Imagination is more important than knowledge." What you visualize enough, you will create in your life.

Now, if you can manifest right out of thin air, then chances are you have another problem. That problem would be not having whatever you create own you. Life is about being owned by the process, not the things or the end result.

The best things in life are free... but the best things in life are NOT things.

Life is about increasing and celebrating your Divine connection with your Higher Self, and the things that you create being a tribute to your Spirit and the Divine process of creation. It is not about replacing your Divine connection with that thing or things you created and forgetting about your Oversoul once you get what you want. This error in priority is what has caused deterioration to society at large. In turn, this deterioration has resulted in serious amnesia about why we are all here and what we are here to do, which is to Divinely connect in the face of the Illusion.

Indigenous tribes have always known this spiritual secret which has been hidden in plain sight to the general population of society. We all must honor the process of creation with our Spirit, our true nature, rather than being owned by the created thing(s). Otherwise, we can really become confused by being disconnected, dysfunctional and/or depressed.

Could you imagine having that much power to create? Right out of the blue? Would you lose your Divine connection enjoying what it is that you created? Would you want to show anyone from an ego standpoint? Typically, the answer is yes. In fact, it is your disconnect that causes your money challenges (or health and relationship challenges too) and is very likely actual evidence of that fact—especially if you are short on or without money right now. Think about that. You are probably owned by all the things you currently have in your life that you created. Now, without money, you could lose them. Maybe, just maybe, this is the way it should be until you realize and get the fact that you were not supposed to lose your Divine connection in exchange for your stuff, circumstances, occasions, persons, and experiences in the first place. Losing your Divine connection is disempowering and actually hinders creating what you want.

Maybe life is continually about being put in a position where you must create.

Integrity is about putting your God/Spirit first in life. I did not say putting the Illusion first. I said putting God first, and God is Love. So if God is Love, then life is about putting Love first, then will second. Maybe you should reread this section on finances and realize that the true meaning of wealth is how few your needs really are.

If you are a billionaire, but you are haunted by worries of who is stealing from you or which investments are scams, you are actually poor because true wealth is in how few your needs really are. Could you be happy with very little? Could you create money and give it all away, realizing that the process of creating was the important piece of the puzzle; and that if you created it once, you could do it again? That is the question you need to think about. It is this Divine process of creation that is key.

After many decades, I now believe that happiness comes before success. You have to learn to be happy where you're at, and true happiness cannot be yours unless you are in gratitude. Entitlement gives you pain, and gratitude will give you ease. I suggest you make a gratitude list of all the things you can be thankful to God for and look at it and add to it every day. And if life has driven you to your knees, it is usually a good place to start getting connected and give gratitude.

The Big Three

Remember, you were created to create and the best way to create is with a peaceful mind. Without a peaceful mind, the fertility of your imagination is very distracted or even eliminated. Your authentic power is in your peace, and your peace provides you with the power to create with your increasingly fertile imagination.

The bottom line is, you must learn how to get to an island of peace within your being, no matter what. This, in turn, will trigger your fertile imagination... and then you can practice creating more and more until you get perfect at it.

Peace is where it's at. Peace is what is required for a fertile imagination. You do NOT want to have a fertile imagination unless you are at peace, as it would fertilize and bring into being all of your fears and worries. All Masters know this. It takes work to get beyond your fears and worries.

∼

The Big Three: Health

Perhaps the word health originally was spelled "WHOLE-TH." Wholeth refers to your entire three-part system of the health of Me, Myself, and I, or Body, Mind and Spirit. True health is about your whole beingness.

Spirit can handle any health issue within the body but the body must have a peaceful mind. If you have a health issue, I will ask, "What is bothering you?" I mean, what is really disturbing you currently? Is it something from your past? Is it something that's bothering you presently, or is it something you are fearful of in the future?

Even though you think you may be finished with your S.C.O.P.E. from your past, you are not complete until you have no emotion wrapped around the dynamics of those issues. Let me be clear; I am not talking about suppressing emotion nor becoming a robot. What I am talking about is growing as a soul, to the point where you are above reacting and those emotions can no longer take you over. You have experienced the ups and the downs many times, and you get to a point where you can observe the situation without being overwhelmed by it. You find yourself responding rather than reacting, from a place of love, while you are in the face of whatever is coming up. This comes with deep understanding and the willingness to see the other side with as much compassion as you see your own point of view. If ever you feel emotion coming up, you know there is something for you to be responsible for, to heal and to get complete with. It is an inner adventure of your own soulful journey to increase your capacity and Love level. No longer is it a victim, pain, and suffering experience of fear.

Your issues are in your tissues. Physical ailments begin in the mental/emotional/spiritual realms. This is good news if you know this information because it will allow you to get beyond where you are having problems. Once you know this, you can clear, clean, forgive, and develop, hopefully to the point of peace. Then your issues will fall away and your tissues will respond in kind.

You may lose the first two of the big three (relationships or money) in your life and recover from those losses, but if you lose your health, you may never recover. Relationships and money can be recoverable or replaceable.

Peace is everything in the health arena. Jesus was known as the Prince of Peace because he knew that a fertile mind comes through peace. We are all here to realize the value of being at peace with our life first, and then we can create the financial wellbeing, the authentic relationships, and the radiant health that we desire to live ideally. Once you get this, it may take you a little while to "complete" the things you thought you were

The Big Three

"finished" with. This is possible through meditation. Meditation will lead you to where it is that you need to be complete. Complete means having no emotions tied to what has happened or is happening. Easier said than done, of course. But by consistent intention, it can be done.

The absolute, ultimate Divine opposite of being a victim is not being a tyrant, but instead being a creator. Contemplate that! Create your dreams beyond what happened or what is happening to you.

You must get to a space where you can go over your life experiences in your meditation and ask your Self, "What was the lesson here?" Eventually, you will see that the event was purposeful for your evolution. You do not have to agree with it but if you ask, you will be shown the meaning of it. Remember, you ultimately must lose the emotion, get the lesson(s), and move on. Life happens for you—not to you. You must get out of the victim mentality if that is where your hang-up is. I can't say this enough, but you absolutely have to lose the emotion to get the real lesson of what happened or what it is happening to you currently. Remember, life happens *for* you... not *to* you.

You first must learn to authentically forgive to get free and complete of where you're at. Not necessarily for the other person's sake, but to get to peace within yourself.

It was the Buddha that said not forgiving someone is like hanging onto a hot coal and expecting the other person to burn.

In the history of the world, nobody has ever died from a snake bite. You read this correctly. You see, if a lion bites you, it could tear your head off. But if a snake bites you, it is usually just two puncture marks in your skin. The bite itself doesn't kill you. It's the poison that flows through your veins, causing your heart and lungs to gradually arrest and quit working that kills you. Not forgiving someone can produce toxins like the snake's poison in your body.

It's surprising how many people will not forgive others because they think that is the way to go. They would much rather hold on to that unforgiveness and be right, as far as they are concerned, than live life itself. That's how crazy life is for some people who are really disconnected.

Have you ever noticed that when you break a relationship with somebody you truly loved, that without that love, you suffer from bouts of insanity? Maybe even a breakdown of health in some form? Love is sanity.

Life is about Love, as Love brings life into assembly. Look at the act of procreation right from conception of the child to birth. You have to agree with me that Love brings everything into assembly because the first item formed in the fetus is the heart. The heart is Love. That heart brought everything else into being. When you think about it, it's absolutely awe-inspiring.

You would think in knowing that Love brings life into assembly, whatever it is that prevents us from not being in tune with Love would be intensely dissolved because we would realize it's a real block. I teach this all the time. People who get this only intellectually, will not fully understand it or live it.

The cells in your body need love and balance to function optimally.

Generally, a person will unwittingly flirt with pushing that balance and love flow while getting the life experience they want or think they need. This can be disastrous if they do not listen to the hiccups that can begin to occur in health as it can snowball into severe health issues.

Often, disease begins with toxicity that has agitated the body to such a degree that disease has formed. This is symbiotic with

The Big Three

what is occurring for a person in their emotional and mental realms. The body is a transcript of the mind. Something in their life has not been loved into an optimum reality, and that S.C.O.P.E. from the past or present is causing so much agitation, it is overwhelming their body/mind system.

Now, the issue is you. Keep that in mind as it is your opportunity to love to a new level and start to "detoxify" your system rather than blame the external dynamics that are occurring.

Generally, whatever is currently disturbing you reflects something that happened in your past or present and is back again to help you take responsibility and improve your ability to be optimized through Divine Love. The reason S.C.O.P.E. leaves your life is that Love jettisons that which is not in tune with it. Sometimes that means you were jettisoned from your S.C.O.P.E., and it isn't just your withdrawal of love from that stuff, circumstances, occasions, persons or experiences.

Life is all about peace. You must be at peace to connect with your God. God is Love. Love is in this world, but it is not *of* this world. Think of Love as the sky. It is various shades of blue from very light to very dark. Our planet is blue and is supported in space in deep blue—True Love.

What is amazing to me is that knowing all this is different from living this truth. To really get it, you must live it. If you don't understand this, then chances are you are living a life in varying degrees of less-than-optimal outcomes and even insanity. Life is Love in action. Don't lose your health over all of the disconnects that you have in your life. No S.C.O.P.E. is worth that. Nothing is worth that. Get back to Peace, get back to Love, get back to God!

So, the Illusion is all about S.H.I.T. for many, many people. How many people say "Shit!" when they are going through major disasters in their relationship, finances, or health? How many people say, "This is shit!" and they don't realize that, yep, it is S.H.I.T. or "Spiritually Harmonizing Intelligent Truth." It is actually the Universe's way of getting you to go within, connect with your Self, and create your way out of it.

How much more pain can you take before you wake up? How do you convert all of these things? These three can interrupt your life and force you to take a look at who you really are and what's important. This is your opportunity to see what you have perpetuated. Then you can start optimally living from a place of Love and courage.

3
WHAT CAN YOU DO TO GET BACK INTO THE DIVINE FLOW?

∽

Now that we have identified ways that the Oversoul is trying to get through to you, let's look at ways you can connect. Connect and get back in the flow with your Spirit and get your spiritual directions and messages by meditating. Listen, you don't have to live your life always on "send". You can be on "receive" by truly connecting and listening in your meditations. You can consciously live your life in a more clear, peaceful, and receptive manner with grace and ease.

This is an important time for you. It is "go time" because wherever you are at right now is magnified. If you are in fear, guilt, shame, anxiety or worry, it is magnified. The only safe place to be is Love and Peace. How do you get to that space? Let's look at that now.

∽

The Way Out Is By Going Within: Meditation

The only way out of the Big Three taxing dynamics is by going within and connecting to Spirit. The routine of doing this is really about the "route in". By going within, I mean learning to meditate to the point of such peace that you can hold one thought in space, in time. Not all the combinations and permutations about one thought, just one thought of something simple. Then ultimately being able to think of nothing without falling asleep. Can you imagine what that would be like?

What if I told you that your purpose on this planet was to become connected to your Spirit? In fact, to actually become *reconnected* to your Spirit because that's the way you came in as a baby. As I have said, the first "sin" was separation. Then the Illusion became the priority for your focus because everyone else was that way. Life is a dream that dreams of Love awakening the human. However, the only way to awaken and stay awake is by becoming reconnected to your Spirit with the understanding of your purpose and performing acts of service and love.

Again, most people suffer from insanity in life because they are so disconnected. It's like everyone kind of knows that this is the problem and that it is happening. But they are asleep and having nightmares in varying degrees, and they can't wake up. As a result, many resort to prescription and recreational drugs, alcohol, food, addiction to electronics, and the pursuit of material things, all to quell the varying degrees of anxiety and depression. That downward spiral in life will eventually lead to more and more destruction and ultimately, death.

The answer is going within and reconnecting with your Spiritual Source. Understanding again that if you don't go within, then you will go without. You will go without your optimized health, the life that you do want, the dreams you desire, and your optimized Divine connection. Successful relationships you really

The Big Three

do want in your life with health, prosperity, and the people you really love, will not happen.

Happiness will be elusive because you do not understand what is required of you and how to get in tune with it. Again, there is no way to happiness because happiness is the way. There are very few teachers that tell you what is exactly required at this time, which is authentic Happiness, Gratitude, Love and Peace. Acceptance of these dynamics is actually essential, as is the true understanding that your transformation is in your acceptance of these dynamics and what life is presenting to you to help you attain a new level of life and priorities.

Jesus was known as the Prince of Peace for a reason. He must have had enormous peace reserves to not react to the public shaming, torture, and all he went through towards the end of his human life. The Kingdom of Heaven is within you. You must understand life is a Divine privilege that provides countless Divine opportunities to evolve. But first, you must transform your understanding of the importance of peace.

There's a difference between change and transformation. Change is what you do for someone else, and as soon as they leave your life, you will revert back to the way that you were. Change is temporary.

Transformation, on the other hand, is permanent. It is what occurs from the cocoon to the butterfly. True transformation occurs whether someone else is around or not because you are not doing it for anybody else other than yourself. This great wave of evolutional transformation is occurring throughout the Universe and is doing so in more and more intense waves. We humans are in a real squeeze right now. We are either on top of this transformational energy wave or under it. That choice is ours because destiny is a matter of choices, not chances. Always choose Love.

Your transformation is in your acceptance.

Everything that is occurring for you right now is perfect for your evolution. Can you honor that? If not, it probably will cause you great misery and, ultimately, death. Eventually, you will see this quite clearly.

So, if you want to live your best life with optimized relationships, finances, and health (starting and primarily with your Oversoul), you must look at your own transformation by accepting what is in front of you currently that perhaps you are not totally comfortable with. But first, it must start with you connecting with your Higher Self, and the best way I have found to do this is through meditation.

Meditation has three parts to it. First, there is prayer. This is where you speak to God. The second is actual meditation where you quiet your mind and God speaks to you. The third is breath. By breath, I mean conscious breath where you learn the techniques of how to create. What you consistently visualize with passion, you will realize and create in your life. Breath is where you create, and remember you were created to create. Breath provides an atmosphere where Spirit connects to matter. This all begins with you quieting your mind.

When you first start the practice of meditation, you will be so polluted with the dynamics of the Illusion that it will seem impossible to just BE. Fear not, is not impossible. Hard yes, but not impossible. "Great," you say, "but how is just sitting on a cushion going to change my life circumstances?" The question is "To BE... or not to BE." What if I told you that if you shift some of your internal perceptions and then truly sit and connect (not just sit there with your eyes closed for 20 minutes or so thinking about all the problems), you really can begin to transform your life in ways you cannot even imagine. Your ultimate destination

The Big Three

in meditation is the Void which is a place of pure Spirit and Nothingness. The idea is to think of nothing without falling asleep.

My meditation practice has an essential element that I call the S-Treatment™ which is integral to meditating more deeply. *Sitting in Stillness and Silence at Sunrise and/or Sunset.* Ideally, outside in nature.

This sacred process, when engaged daily, really enhances the Presence of your inner voice. The process itself provides more space and time in life to sit and listen to your heart and your Oversoul. By practicing this discipline, you begin to understand the phrase "Be still and know that I am God."

Silence is indivisible—it is the space between the words we speak. Your growth is obtained and sustained in silence.

Sunrise represents new beginnings, while sunset is about balance and represents the "even-ing" of your day.

After witnessing many sunrises and sunsets on a regular basis, I assure you, you will be hooked. It will become an essential part of who you are.

Master's Motto: Do Nothing (the Void) and accomplish everything.

An optimized life is an inside job.

You must remember, life happens for you, not to you. If you don't get this, your relationships, finances and health will be stormy to the point of collapse until you are left without anything. Perhaps then you will choose to go within. If you don't go within and get reconnected, you will go without authentic happiness, peace and Love.

The bottom line is that your Oversoul will meet you at every dead-end, even if you have to die to do it. As such, you best believe how important connecting with your Spirit and listening to it really is. Right now, wherever you're at in your life is magnified. Again, if you are in fear, guilt, shame, anxiety and worry, it is magnified. I can't say this enough right now; the only safe place to be is Love and Peace. Look for the best in all your S.C.O.P.E.

So, you had best get comfortable at meditating and building a relationship with your Higher Self, in proportion to the amount you want to stop the insanity in your life and start enhancing your relationships, financial situation, and health via peace. And start loving and living your best life!

Whatever your choice is, I wish you enough.

∼

Don't Judge

A lot of times, we can see this in other people's lives. It is easy to see how if that friend would just respect herself/himself more, their intimate relationships and other things would be different. Or if that other friend would only become more responsible, their world would open up and that relationship problem or that financial situation would completely clear up. But it is never that easy to see our own issues and that the same principles apply to us. There is always a lesson to learn from our financial woes, our health situation, or our relationship dramas. As easy as it is to point the finger and blame our S.C.O.P.E., the only way out is to realize that you need to focus solely on the lesson that is showing up for you.

In a retrospective view of life, you have to agree that a positive circumstance quite often becomes a negative circumstance, and

The Big Three

the reverse can be true as well. If you come to this conclusion, you will see that life is purposeful. Incidences are neutral; it's the perception charge that we put on them that makes them polarized. Life is all about alchemy, where issues that are negative turn out to be positive, and vice versa.

If you are in a difficult spot right now, it may seem like the end of the world. But if you look at the many examples in society where people were at their lowest and turned things around, it shows what is possible. Often it's because they got connected in one way or another. They listened, got the lesson they were being shown, and created anew.

In fact, your life is like film photography. You develop from the negative so the negative is necessary – as is the positive. Many people come to me with negative things and say, "Well, look, this is awful," and I say, "What an opportunity to create! This problem shall pass." If you look back at your life, many of the positive incidents became negative, and quite a few of the negative incidents eventually became positive. When something initially happens, an event/incident, who are we to say whether it is positive or negative? Contemplate that.

I tell a story about the donkey and the father. This tale goes back in time to the 1500s. It is a late August day. The father is sitting on the veranda of his farmhouse, and his son is over to the right sitting in a chair. The father is in his rocking chair smoking his pipe. It's very hot out. He is looking at the crop. It is the best crop he has ever had.

The wind is blowing softly. He sees the crop waving in the wind and realizes that it is probably God waving at him. He smiles.

His son is there, but his wife is not because she died and crossed over to the other half of the sky when giving birth to their son. So, it has just been him and his now 15-year-old son all this time.

He loves his son very much. He realizes that the crop will soon be taken off with his son and his donkey's assistance. He looks over there at the donkey; the donkey is young and so strong. Without that donkey and his son, he probably would not be able to get most of his crop off. But they can definitely get it all off with all the three of them.

The time is fast approaching for harvest. Maybe another week. The sun is streaming on them all; it is 80 degrees F. The sky is clear, life is good, and the father realizes he is in the heights of happiness.

However, the very next day, the donkey goes missing. Oh my God, thought the father, the donkey is gone. They search high and low for this donkey for a week. No trace. The father does not know how he is going to pull that crop off now. He would have to scythe it off by hand with his son. My goodness, they probably would not get half of the crop off without the donkey. And the father goes from the heights of happiness to the depths of despair.

This is a disaster. He is devastated.

The following day, the donkey returns with a white Arabian stallion in tow. The stallion is in love with the donkey. This Arabian stallion is worth more than the crop, the house, and everything else that the farmer has. The father goes from the depths of despair to the heights of happiness.

The following week, his son is riding the white Arabian stallion and gets kicked off. He lands and he breaks his hip. Although the donkey is back, without the son, they are only going to get a little more than half of this crop off if they are lucky. Never mind the fact that his son will have a limp for the rest of his life. And the father goes from the heights of happiness to the depths of despair because his son has a crippling injury.

The Big Three

The following week, the militia came to town and conscripted all boys, 14 and above, for the war with the exception of his son due to his hip injury. And the father went from the depths of despair to the heights of happiness because very few young soldiers returned from war as they were sent to the front lines with no hope of survival.

What is the moral of the story?

Don't judge. It's not over 'til it's over, and it is actually never over, especially when you factor in reincarnation. This cautionary tale is something to contemplate.

As soon as you realize that life is an infinite series of positives and negatives, you should have joy. From the viewpoint of simultaneous polarities, your life will improve because you can see that life is purposeful. You may not always understand why something is happening, but it is happening for a purpose, and possibly your evolution. So, do not judge. Again, life happens *for* you, not *to* you.

If you are up against one or more of the Big Three, see this as a huge opportunity for you to transform, to connect with your Higher Self on a whole new level, and possibly evolve to a higher level of you. Remember, when you change the way you look at things... the things you look at change. Will it be hard? Most likely, but so is life when learning to walk, swim or ride a bike. Once you master perception, you will feel a new level of freedom and excitement that can be indescribable! Life is hard until it isn't.

∼

Harmonize, Harness, and Convert

What can someone do when faced with a good dumping of the Big Three in their life? It is called the H.H.C. principle: Harmonize, Harness and Convert.

How are you going to convert your life dynamics to your benefit? The Teaching. This H.H.C. principle is like a lot of the martial arts that Shaolin monks are taught. They learn three ways to take an incoming blow. One is to take it right there in the head – "BAM." The second way is to step aside and watch as it goes "WHOOSH" right past them. The third is to capture the incoming blow, redirect that energy, and force it back in on itself by converting the energy. Just as they can convert the energy, so can you. Just convert the energy of all of the S.H.I.T. in your life with Love, and you will gain access to a higher order of life, peace, and creativity through conversion as you lose the fear with the principle of Love first, will second. This is because everything in the Illusion initially comes from Love, then decays and returns to Love. Love is in this world, but not of this world. Love is the great converter. However, you must understand that it's not about who is right but what is right, as the basis of Love.

Wouldn't it be great to learn how to do life in a new way with various spiritual techniques and philosophies? You will then be tested and tested because once I teach you this, you are going to get tested in your life.

You will get tested until:

1. In the face of the hardships, you DON'T forget to use what you have just learned, and DON'T revert back to your old way of doing things (including pain), **or**

2. You use what you have learned here to take your evolution to a new level. Thought determines what you want, but action determines what you get.

That choice is yours. Life will teach you what is right. I just have to teach you the philosophy; that is my gift to you. Then you get to use what you have learned in experience because experience is truth in many different dimensions.

The Tools To Evolve

In life, the Teaching provides you with life tools. That being said, you should know that everything we teach you about the tools does not work.

So why would anyone want to take the Teaching from me or anyone else, you may ask? Well, let me tell you about the tools. They are a lot like a saw, a nail gun, a hammer, etc. Tools will not work by themselves. You have to pick up the tool, and you have to use it. Then it will work. Tools work the same way as The Teaching; you have to use them in order for them to work. Otherwise, it is just a tool sitting there, just a philosophical discussion piece unless you choose to apply it in the face of your life's circumstances.

Let's say you are a first generation, primitive man, and you are hammering wooden nails in with your stone, and I come along from the future, and I introduce to you a steel-head hammer, and you go, "Wow, what a great tool!" and life really changes for you—if you use it.

I see this in people that I teach. They come back six months later; despite receiving the tool, they have dropped the hammer and have gone back to using their stone. And I ask them, "How is that working for you?"

They reply, metaphorically, "Well, I experienced quite a bit of pain, but look at what I built." And the truth of the matter is that they didn't build much of anything very well, and on top of it all, they damaged themselves.

These tools that you are learning here must be used regularly for them to really work. If you don't want to use what I am teaching you, you will not get out from under the load of any of the Big Three. Although these tools will make your life easier if you use them, they will only make your life harder if you don't. Experience is truth.

The idea here is to lessen life's pain, not increase it. The amount of S.H.I.T. in your life will probably increase until you do use these tools. It is called the burden of truth.

Ignorance is forgivable; knowingness is not... on this and the other half of the sky. If you know better and keep doing it the old way, the heat could get turned up in the dynamics of your life. This is why your Divine integrity whispers to you from your heart, and often you know what the best choice is for you at the moment. There is no punishment counsel deciding your fate and/or worth on the other half of the sky. God does not judge you on the other half of the sky because God is Love. Judging is a human trait. Evolution is about cause, effect, and soulful evolution.

Let me give you further clarity; the Universe has an unending supply of S.H.I.T. just for you. It is not going to end until you consciously use these Spiritual tools. One of you is going to run out of gas, and it's not going to be the Universe. Using the tools can be very difficult, a significant challenge. But by not using them, life ranges from difficult to impossible. So, you can choose hard or impossible. Again, conscious choices often involve risk, but if you don't risk doing this, you risk even more—your life. Life is about soulful, sacred evolution.

So how much more of this S.H.I.T. can you take in life? Most people can only take so much, and then they think/say, "I can't handle this, I'm gonna get ill, I'm out of here." And I say, "Ok, that's your call, but you know what you will have to get through, even if it's in the next lifetime."

You probably know in life what soulful classes you have been taking and what lessons you are working on. It's all about your soul's evolution. You have in front of you an ideal set of circumstances that were tailor-made for your evolution... but you must go within.

Meditate, meditate, meditate.

I can never say that enough. If not, you will go back to sleep again in the Illusion, just sleepwalking around. If someone doesn't wake you up, rest assured life will.

Could your true understanding of all this be the purpose of you reading this? As soon as you go unconscious with respect to your spiritual evolution, if you haven't noticed, the road gets bumpier and the speed bumps become more severe. In fact, you can hit the odd 50-foot wall, where you just can't get around it. Life is meant to squeeze you so that you go within and find your Divine connection. Maybe the spiritual squeeze in the Illusion is supposed to happen until you understand what I am teaching you. So, where are you getting squeezed to wake up right now? Relationships? Finances? Health? Which one? All three?

Remember, life happens *for* you, not *to* you. If you get this, your life changes.

Your transformation is in your acceptance. If you are going to transform anything, you have to accept it for what it is first, and then you can change it by using Harmonize, Harness, Convert. So, understand your transformation is in your acceptance, even though sometimes you do not understand why. Just accept it. To optimize your life, you will need to use this H.H.C. tool.

It took me decades to understand that my transformation was in my acceptance because I did not want to accept S.H.I.T. unless I first understood why.

"Tell me why first, and then I will accept it."

The Oversoul said, "No, I'll tell you when you can accept it, and you will understand why then. Sometimes it is before, but for you, it is going to have to be after."

And would say, "WHY?!?"

And my Oversoul replied, "Because of the way that you are, right now."

"Really? Is that negotiable?" I said.

And the reply was, "No."

That took my breath away. But when the Oversoul said, "*NO*" (I am going to change your mind right here), the Oversoul spelled it KNOW (even though I initially took it as NO).

KNOW. And then I was taught, "When you change the way you look at things, the things you look at change."

I had to *know* that this was the way of learning the necessity of connecting spiritually. The Oversoul was not saying *no*; she/he was saying *know*.

Shortly after I got that, I realized it was the nudge I needed to actually connect and *know* that my spiritual connection was required. Subsequently, I really understood why it had to happen that way in the Illusion. It was for me to truly connect with my Oversoul.

The Big Three

Integrity

If you live with enough integrity, you will never be lost—for long. You will not experience as much S.H.I.T... well, not as much as you could have!

Integrity is how you live and what you do when no one is watching.

Integrity is putting your God first, and God is Love. Life is all about opportunities for Love first, will second.

Ultimate Integrity is ultimate Spirit and that is ultimate Love. They are ultimately equal, and these qualities are natural within a young child unless the child has been taught otherwise. Jesus spoke of becoming like a child to enter the Kingdom of Heaven. Integrity is one of the main properties of being a young child; it is natural until they become tainted by the Illusion.

Integrity bonds and conversely, things fall apart without integrity. Integrity is the energy of Love, and transparency is its child. Pure Love has no disguise. When the integrity is gone in your car fender, it rusts; if integrity is wearing out in the concrete on the bridge, the concrete flakes and cracks. When the integrity is gone in a business or a personal relationship, it too falls apart. People just start speaking past each other. Integrity is essential in life. Earth is an integrity school.

So what class are you currently taking in integrity school on the planet? Love 101? Peace 202? Perception 303? Compassion 404? We are all taking classes at different levels in the integrity school of this planet.

Life Happens For Us, Not To Us

Life happens for us, not to us. I cannot say this enough. "Life is a great thing—if it doesn't kill you." This is one of my favorite dining toasts. It is the irony of life, you know. We all have each other on loan for a little while. After all, we are all walking each other home. Everyone that you have on your stage in life is there to help you evolve. Look at all of the current people you have in supporting roles helping you to evolve. Each of us has this phantasmagoria of events happening in our life. Who arranged all of these dynamics with all the stuff, circumstances, occasions, persons, and experiences that you have in your life, perfectly in place, just for you to evolve? It was/is your Oversoul!

I am here to remind you, and I will say this over and over again... you are a spiritual being having a human experience, not the other way around. Most people think that they are a human having an occasional spiritual experience. How you see it is up to you. Perception is everything. Is it possible that you could recognize and agree you are a spiritual being having a human experience and that perhaps during your human experience, you got hurt and you withdrew love?

When you get to the other half of the sky, do you know what's interesting? The system is set up to do a life review, and it becomes obvious where you withdrew love. Often times you had an ulterior motive, and you did not tell the total truth because you wanted something in particular to occur that you had an undeclared interest in. When you get to the other half of the sky, the life review dynamics that really stand out are where you had an ulterior motive. When you have an ulterior motive, you are not in integrity, and life starts to chip away at you from that point on. Things do not work out optimally, and that is where life eventually really disappoints you as your relationships and more begin to fall apart. Why? Because, as I said previously, things fall apart without integrity. And integrity is putting your

The Big Three

God first... and God is Love. Listening to the voiceless voice whispering within you is when you "know" you are living in integrity.

How many more of the same disappointing situations do you have to go through? Even though the people change, your reoccurring circumstances don't, because you are supposed to learn something and you haven't. As I have said, the definition of insanity is doing the same thing over and over again and expecting a different result. Another way to look at it is, "If I always do what I have always done, I will always get what I have always got." This is a very famous quote by Henry Ford, and he is absolutely correct.

Spirit arranges all of the phantasmagorias of S.H.I.T. for each one of us to evolve. If you are lucky like I was, you find a true spiritual teacher that leads you to understand this, so you can appreciate why your S.H.I.T. happened. A true spiritual teacher is without judgment, understands, and leads you to your center, which is your way out. All of life is purposeful, whether you agree with it or not.

Do you know what smart people do? They learn from their mistakes. Do you know what geniuses do? They learn from other people's mistakes. You do not have to recreate the wheel. You can hang out with a bunch of people who have good spiritual values and find a teacher that is not about "drinking the Kool-Aid." Find an authentic spiritual teacher who says you need to take a hard look at your belief systems and which ones don't work for you anymore. Find a teacher who will say, "I am not perfect. But I can and will show you a few of the roads to get back home to yourself."

The Teaching is not about control; other than that you have to control your habit of going along with your Ego/Act. Instead, listen to your Oversoul to advance your evolution. In order to gain control of life, you must give up control. Trust. Surrender.

But don't give up. That paradox of life is worth a lot of contemplation. Can you have a commanding Presence in life without being controlling? Yes. It's a matter of where you are coming from, your Spirit or your Ego/Act.

∼

Conscious Choices

Have you ever noticed that your life is pretty cyclical, with similar situations that keep coming up, often with the same people and circumstances, or sometimes with other people? That's because you keep getting the opportunity to make different choices, conscious choices that are in tune with the whisper of your Oversoul. To be humbled enough to do what is right in the situation or to have the integrity to say no, even though it may cost you a relationship and/or money.

Controlling other people will not optimize your life. If you want to gain control in your life, you have to give up control, and then your life transforms. Again, "When you change the way you look at things, the things you look at change." Trust... it's that simple.

It's not how you start off in life; it's how you end at your transition to the other half of the sky. None of us can go back and create a brand-new beginning, but if you truly get life, you can become conscious *now* and create a brand-new end. This is a direct result of you beginning to make conscious choices. Conscious choices are not reactionary choices; they are responsive choices. Reaction is typically about emotional choices. Responsive choices are usually about un-emotional responsible choices of Love first, will second. It's not really about who is right, but what is right. It is not just what is good for you; it's the best for all concerned. And if we have a planet that thinks just this way, what happens to the world? Amazing

The Big Three

things. There are more and more amazing pockets of people who resonate with this way of being. As they tune into this philosophy, they find that they transform and life around them transforms as well. Sometimes people completely transform their lives when they realize that their gate, their exit off this plane, may come sooner rather than later, and they start living consciously, NOW. It's like the Buddhist philosophy, "Every member of humanity always thinks they have more time." Act now, like there is no tomorrow, on the things that really matter... especially your primary life's purpose which is to re-ignite your Divine relationship on this half of the sky before you cross back to the other side.

Destiny is not a matter of chance; it is a matter of choices.

It is a matter of starting to make conscious choices. It's not just I, me, mine; what's good for me? No, you want to get beyond that mindset because you want to make a difference in the world. You do this by finding your Higher Self. As you find your Higher Self, you can assist others.

All authentic teachers know this, and they do this selflessly. They assist others. We are all walking each other home. In order to give to someone else, you have to have something to give. If you are emotionally and spiritually bankrupt, you have nothing to give. That is what started me on this path. I was ground down to zero, emotionally and spiritually. I decided that I could not be in this world that way anymore, so I studied spirituality for seven years. I was taught by a Master in a foreign land—it was pretty cool. I then went and sat in the trees and I subsequently was re-calibrated with the right life priorities and values over time.

I came back to Canada almost as a foreigner to society. My psychic antennas were way more extensive than before. Walking through the streets, I could hear people's thoughts. And I wondered, "Oh, wow, why do most think such toxic and judgmental thoughts about themselves and others?" So, it became another journey for me to get past this judgment dynamic itself.

There is no quantum jump in your evolution unless there is risk. Quite often, conscious choices are risky and can result in the loss of money and/or image. Believe me, it was a real risk for me to take that time off. But in fact, I had no choice as I was insane in the Illusion. You have to decide if you are going to put credits in your Higher Self bank account or in your image account with other humans. Worrying about what others will think of you will not get you optimized, it will just make you confused because you are not in integrity with your Higher Self.

Loving, conscious choices are really where it's at in life. It is the apex point where you can evolve to the highest form of Love and Peace of Being as the pinnacle objective of your life and with life on the planet. You can progressively live your best life.

Be at peace with all, and you will access a whole different Universe. You may want to read the classic poem Desiderata —the message is profound and is a pretty good guide to life.

Love jettisons that of which is not in tune with it. As you make more conscious choices, loving your Higher Self more, be prepared for some S.C.O.P.E. to leave your life. No S.C.O.P.E. is worth giving up the kingdom of heaven for. But you must also be responsible with that perception. Once again, pure Love is an energy, not an emotion—human love is emotion.

∼

Your Power Is In Your Peace

So all of us have our final life gate; it's called death. It is also known as our transition, and that transition is typically a

The Big Three

beautiful event. The thing about death is that it's a wake-up call. Death wakes you up, either when you are dying or for the ones you leave behind. The traditions for those who have passed are called a "wake" for a reason—they are meant to wake us up —that's the irony of it.

I mean really, what is death? Death is just a point where dying stops anyways. If you think about it, we are all here for only a little while. You are here to find and reconnect with your Higher Self, your Oversoul, right in the middle of a fairway of "the greatest indoor show on earth." Finding your Higher Self and connecting is your true life purpose. What you do for a living is usually different. All of us lose our Higher Selves in order to find or rediscover our Higher Selves—it's a fact. You get clarity through contrast; you find out who you are—by realizing who you are not. You appreciate water by not having any, food by not having any, love by not having any, peace by not having any. This is a world of opposites, and when you get real clarity through contrast, you realize a good relationship from a bad relationship (a toxic relationship). You realize the value of peace.

It is your choice to review this book as many times as it takes to quench what you are looking for and open the door to truth. That door is always open. That door is yours to walk through. It's a great place to get to as it ultimately leads to more and more Peace and Love. This all starts with meditation for longer and longer periods of time and eventually being at peace with everything in your life... and all of life.

All the greats knew the value of Peace. What if I told you that sustained peace is a way of being that triggers a fertile imagination? That is how Initiates become Masters. It is through Peace, Love, Focus and Gratitude. When optimized, you just think about something, and it comes to be. If you are at peace, your incidents of co-incidence can go up. And it can go up from there... beyond co-incidents to synchronicity.

Wouldn't it be great to have a daily life filled with co-incidents where life dynamics just line up and occur for you every day, every week, month, and year? Life would then just happen magically. You just think about it, and it comes into being. Can you imagine experiencing that more and more often?

That is the way life is supposed to be, but for most, life is "pushing the river" as I call it. If you are "pushing the river," you are not going to win. If you are "pushing the river," the Universe is giving you a pipeline of S.H.I.T. and hopefully, after a while, you get the picture. If not, life becomes impossible. Either you go inside (coincide) or you go insane, and you will think about quitting and possibly even starting to consider leaving the planet. But if you can harmonize, harness, and convert the challenging dynamics of your life starting right now and begin to create a life of ever-increasing conscious, loving, present moments, you may get to your transition point and look back at the beauty of your life—all of your life—and how perfectly it unfolded to get you to connect with your Spirit and find peace within yourself.

∼

Childlike Properties

Now, if in receiving this information, you don't have a laugh or a chuckle at some point when looking back at the way you have been, you are probably experiencing a not too optimized life to varying degrees of outright insanity. And one of the most effective ways to counter this is with childlike properties such as laughter. Childlike properties are a large part of The Teaching. As I've said, Jesus was right when he said you must become like a child to enter the Kingdom of Heaven.

What does that really mean? Well, you must have these properties of Love, Innocence, Being the Observer, Light

The Big Three

Heartedness, Integrity, and you must have Trust and Presence. If you remember, you came here with these properties naturally. They got hammered out of you by your S.C.O.P.E. They were knocked out of you by the Illusion to the point where you lost these childlike properties to varying degrees. This is because you put the Illusion first in life and not your Spirit. This is because no one taught you better. Trust, Presence, Light Heart (laughter), Integrity, Love, Innocence were dissipated to eventually being mostly all gone. Judgment became the norm and at that point, you could no longer fully enjoy life. Without childlike properties, life can be incredibly draining. Typically, you are too busy judging and complaining. If this rings true for you, how is that working out for you? When I hear people's stories about their lives, I say to them, "How is life working for you?" Most often, the answer is, "Not very well. Insane, actually."

No matter how successful you are or are not in life, usually you know something is missing because you are missing these childlike properties. These properties can produce magic. When these properties are regained, they also produce Peace and Love regardless of your external success. These are the true benchmarks of a successful Divine life. These properties are key at a time where this energy wave of excess is rolling through the Universe. There is something within you that knows you cannot miss this energy wave in this life, out of all of your lifetimes. This is a pinnacle wave for you, and something within you knows this in a noticeably big way... and that is why a lot of people are feeling the anxiety that they are.

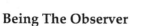

Being The Observer

Consciousness is my server, as long as I am the Observer

God is the ultimate Observer. The Observer is neutral. God is pure Love, and that Love is an energy... not an emotion. Human love is typically conditional and is emotional.

I have said to myself countless times over the years, "Consciousness is my server, as long as I am the Observer."

So, you know, part of life is learning that judging another is useless; it's a waste of life. You have to understand the difference between judging and observing. Judging typically means you think less of the person or thing. Observing is seeing that it is what it is.

Let's say I'm holding a coffee mug. I don't judge it. It is what it is. Do I say, "Oh, it's probably cheap material in there, probably flimsy and breakable, uh, look at this, I think it should be bigger and designed much better." What a waste of time judging is. The mug is what it is. Judging gets a lot of free rent in our heads that we could be using for space to be the Observer and create.

If I give you a 1000-page book, and I say, "Read one page." Can you actually tell what the book is about? No. When you judge someone, you are typically only getting one or a few pages of who they are. The only entity that is qualified to judge (and it does not) is the Oversoul. By looking at one page of a 'book' (possibly the worst thing the person has ever done in their life), for you to judge that person is a waste of life. Everyone is doing what they need to do to get to where they need to be. Everybody is. Everyone is figuring out who they are by who they are not. Let them be, for God's sake. Look how long it took you to get to what you are being taught, right here. Whoa. If that doesn't give you a new perception of life and increase your compassion for others, then I don't know what will. Expect more of the same S.H.I.T. that you are going through until you finally say, "Ok, I will not judge." Well, as your teacher, I wish you enough.

The Big Three

Judging causes the first 'sin' which is separation from your Oversoul. You become disempowered. So, when you learn the principle of replacing judging another with being the Observer, you are into a whole different domain of reality. Can you practice being the Observer? Again, consciousness is my server as long as I am the Observer.

God is the ultimate Observer. Life is about aligning yourself with that power.

Your Divinity is in your tranquility. Tranquility is not a bedfellow with judging; you have to learn to be the Observer—no judging. You can still observe and make decisions without judging. As long as you have been judging, tell me the moments that it made you a better person. It hasn't, has it? You can observe and make conscious choices. Stick with that. What un-conscious judging has probably done is gotten you into a whole bunch of unnecessary dramas.

You know, there is a Monk by the name of Brother David that I really like, and I am going to suggest you listen to a specific recording by him that I enjoy. Locate it on YouTube, "*A Good Day*" with Brother David Steindl-Rast, and listen to it. It begins with, "You think this is just another day in your life? It's not just another day."

The recording is about being graceful with life and appreciating it for what it is, and not complaining about what it is not. Life is so special. Even after all these years, I question all the time if even I can see as much beauty as there really is in life. I take a look at the mountains, the sunrise, the sunset—am I truly appreciating all that it is?

You might be surprised as to how many people who know that they are about to leave this plane in their final two or three days, and they plead for just one more sunrise. "God, please give me another sunrise." Sometimes that wish is granted, and sometimes that gift is not. But perhaps the Oversoul says, "And how many sunrises did you take in when the opportunity was yours?" And most people would have to say, "Not enough, I was busy." Caught in the busy-ness of life, head down-bum up, caught up in life's dramas on so many things and didn't take the time to smell the roses or watch the sunrises along the way.

Chances also are you probably never said I love you enough to people that meant the most to you. Your Mom, your Dad, your Brothers, your Sisters. Even amidst the turmoil and the family dissension. It doesn't matter. What matters is Love. That is what matters.

∼

The Inside World

So, you came in with these childlike properties and, because of how society is and how we were raised, no one taught you that the inside world is more important than the outside world of man-made things. If you had been my child, I would have told you repeatedly, "The inside world is more important than the outside world of man-made things. And if you lose that, you are going to lose your connection to your Source... and that means insanity."

Now, the outside world of *non-man-made* things—like the sky, the clouds, the sun, the moon, the stars, the trees, the mountains —that's stuff in the outside world that you *should* look at and think about the beauty of it. If you were my child, I would tell you that insanity happens when too much man-made stuff gets in your eye aperture, if that is all you are focusing on in life with your S.C.O.P.E.

The Big Three

Have you ever really made serious time for the non-man-made stuff? If not, you probably lost your way, became confused, and you suffered from bouts with one or more of the Big Three. Maybe, if you found a teacher that taught you about S.H.I.T. early enough and long before you got to your gate at the end of your life, you would be able to make something of this life that really matters. Not your net worth financially, I am talking about net worth spiritually. Spiritual capital, the stuff that makes things go around, makes sanity happen and makes confusion stop. If you are still alive, you have the opportunity to become conscious.

Most people are going through taxing dynamics right now on the planet. The circumstances that you have in your life are probably guiding or driving you to go to your center. These circumstances will continue until you go to your center and get connected to God, whatever definition you put on God. As I have said, for me, God is the Grand Over-All Designer. That's where G.O.D. makes sense to me.

Who designed all this, for "God's sake"? The Universe, this planet, all the plant life, all the systems of life. Really who designed all this? What surpasses that? Honestly, it should take your breath away. You look at the oceans; they have been there since the beginning of life. They have been around for eons. Oceans, "Oh-see-the-eons." We speak a language we do not understand. That is one of our biggest problems. That is what communion is all about—common union with our Oversoul, 'Communion.' Again, we speak a language we do not understand.

As you wake up, you get to see all these things that you never saw before, you are waking up, and you will cry as I did. I started crying at one point in my life when I began to realize how precious and beautiful life really is… and I cried in bouts, off and on for two-and-a-half years. My wife and I would be out for supper, and I would start crying deeply, as though my mother had just died. And my wife would say, "What?"

And I would say, "Everything is just so beautiful." So, I finally went within, and I said to my spiritual team, my God, "Why do I cry?"

And the Oversoul said, "Because you are finally here, you understand the purpose, perfection and beauty of everything. You finally understand. Life is so magnificent in its evolution and is so beautiful. It also makes you sorry that other people don't get it like you do and you cry."

I said, "Thank you." And the bouts of crying continued; it would happen every day, sometimes more than once a day. Because I got it, I was happy, yet I was sad. There is a statement that I finally understood; live to the point of tears. I finally understood it. I was in my heart and my Oversoul was now getting in.

So, all of your circumstances that are all around you are getting you to go within. Surrender to your God is my advice, but don't give up. Have faith and have a little fun along the way! Focus on connecting to deeper and deeper depths.

∽

Your Opportunity Is Here, Now

Priorities have to change in your life because this is your time to transform. The invisible (Spirit) is more important than the visible (the Illusion), and you must believe in the invisible to do the impossible. This is why you came to this planet at this time, and you know it. You were created to create. What problems do you have if you can create? Contemplate that for a long time and see what happens to your reality.

The Big Three

The realization and application of this knowledge is your most significant opportunity in life. What if I told you that if you are reading this, *this is your time*. Do you think you can open this book and not be woken up and stirred? If you are not stirred here, this book is not for you because this book is here to wake you up. I teach people, and they often get choked up and they cry, in a good way, because you know what? They realize this is close to their spiritual home.

This teaching speaks to my heart, it speaks to my very soul, and I genuinely hope that it speaks to yours as well. In reading this book, you may have experienced what I call the shrills. Shrills are goosebumps on top of goosebumps, aka 'God bumps.' It feels like "Oh my God"—and that is precisely the right statement. These shrills are meant to provide you with a state of Presence and Spirit is saying, "Pay attention here." These moments signify that you have read or heard something that feels true to you at the very depths of your being.

The truth shall set you free, but first it is going to make you cry. I had that with my teacher too, and I knew I was in the right spot and that my questions had been answered. I knew I had hit the motherload of truth, and I am thankful to this day. Thank you to my Teacher and my God.

It all started as my life spiralled down and out of control, and I looked up to the sky and asked, "Can anyone make sense of what is going on here on Earth?" Finally, I found the answer to that question—through my Teacher and then The Teaching itself.

My teacher didn't look like a Master. It took me two years to realize that he actually was one. I was so defensive. Never mind appearances; he sure didn't look like what I thought a Master should look like. But I am eternally grateful that I put judgment aside and stayed the course and listened to the truth. As a result, I started living truth—long enough to be a teacher. It is the reason I can share with you what I have learned.

You know it's a funny thing about The Teaching, an important element required for it is something I say to many students, "May you listen as well as you hear." You see, your ears hear perfectly; listening is what gets in. If you have a child around you or if you have had a child, you will have a moment I'm sure where you say, "Look, you are not listening to me." They hear you, but what really matters is what gets in. So, I am blessing you with *may you listen as well as you hear*. May these words echo in the canyons of your soul as you read them. If so, maybe I can help make some sense out of life for you. Wouldn't that be great? You could actually walk around smiling again and recapture that feeling of freedom and joy that you experienced as a child—enjoying each moment of the adventure called life, more than you ever have, in greater and greater waves.

The whole journey of life is sacred; it is about getting to your spiritual center. And then maybe you will find and get taught by a Master Teacher. A teacher who will make you realize what you have been failing to see all this time. Just like looking into the stereogram type of 3D art you used to find in the malls. The pictures within the picture of the ocean floor with a bunch of sea creatures. But you must get past the surface art to do so. The process of going within is itself an art. Proof that when you change the way you look at things, the things you look at change.

A Master Teacher will teach you first how to connect via meditation more and more deeply. That is the start of your new journey.

Over time, this gets less daunting and becomes your new normal. I too am a spiritual being having a human experience. I knew when I found my teacher because learning from him was like drinking from a fire hose. That is what happens when you are ready. And all of a sudden, it is like, "Oh my God, I get it!"

And there, you will find freedom.

I invite you to read my series of books about going further in-depth on the topics I have touched on above. I also have an online community where you can learn and share and grow your spiritual connection. www.TheCFT.ca

I look forward to possibly sharing the journey more... much more, with you. It is quite an adventure.

I would love to hear from you as to your thoughts on what I have written here for you.

Love and Blessings.

I AM, in all humility,

Zalah

∼

ABOUT THE AUTHOR

∼

I do my best to help people make sense of life because, for many, the load of life is just too much right now. You are led to what you need to know when you need to know it. It's about you recognizing that in life. That is how people are led to me as a teacher. People find a teacher when they finally get to the point where they think, "Can anybody make any sense out of all of this? Life is confusing. It's driving me crazy. Why can't I enjoy life?!" That's what happened to me... and many like me. I went searching for the true meaning of life.

This teaching is not about religion, nor is it my teaching. It's the Wisdom of the Ages, actually. I just teach it. It is my truth, and I own it by living it at the highest level that I possibly can. Am I perfect? No. Life is a process that does not end... not even at death. Death is a comma, not a period.

I am nothing great, I am not special, I am unique. Just like a thumbprint. I am just an ordinary guy that has done a lot of studying of spiritual matters and has had some incredible incidents of Spiritual confirmations which some would call outright miracles. I truly understand what Jesus meant when he said, "What I can do, yee can do also, and more."

If you are emotionally and spiritually bankrupt, you have

nothing to give to life. That's what started me on this path —probably just like you. I was emotionally unavailable, spiritually I had no values, and I decided I couldn't be that way anymore. I had nothing to give life. In fact, I would say I was insane.

Life is a trade-off, and at that time, I had only taken and I had nothing to give. So, I took off seven years for spiritual studies. I went and sat in the trees and was taught by a Master in another land. I tell people that I am a true Rhodes Scholar (spelled R-O-A-D-S) because life experience is the path to truth.

In my prior life within this lifetime, I went to excess. But when I found the spiritual path, I went to excess too. I found that the path to excess actually led me to the palace of wisdom. That is what happened to me. Now I do not expect you to be fanatical, but wow, I learned a lot by sitting in stillness and silence in the trees for a long time. I don't tell people how long because they may never talk to me again, out of fear. Can you imagine sitting there in nature long enough that thoughts of your life back there in society—of all your stuff, circumstances, occasions, persons, experiences (S.C.O.P.E.)—all stop? Can you imagine?

Many of the roles I played in this life have simply become fodder for my growth and evolution (fodder for the true experience and understanding of what I share with you in these pages) and is no longer who I am today. Through the tough initiation called life, studying under a Master Teacher for seven years, and my focused time in nature with my Divine, it is now possible for me to be this copper wire that I am, for the service of humanity and the health of the planet today.

I AM humbled and honored to share the Wisdom of the Ages with you.

Thank you for the privilege of my being a part of your evolutionary journey and for allowing me to share my truth with you.

I AM, humbly,
Zalah

∼

ALSO BY ZALAH

The Secret of Creation

Caught in The Act

CPSIA information can be obtained
at www.ICGtesting.com
Printed in the USA
LVHW091128020421
683298LV00003B/437